THE GREAT BIG IRISH ANNUAL 2021

Gill Books

THIS BOOK BELONGS TO

NAME ....

ADDRESS ....

AGE ....

CONTENTS

Welcome to

~~~

THE GREAT BIG IRISH ANNUAL 2021

INSIDE, YOU'LL FIND ...

LOTS OF FUN THINGS TO MAKE AND DO

CRAZY FACTS AND SILLY SCIENCE

HECTIC HISTORY AND SERIOUS SPORTS

... AND MUCH, MUCH MORE.

so jump in!

This is **YOUR BOOK**. You can **SCRIBBLE ON IT, MESS IT UP, CUT PAGES OUT**, and **EVEN CHEW ON IT** (well, we'd prefer if you didn't do that).

YOUR BEST BITS

The year 2020 was a pretty crazy time for everyone. **How was your year?**

MY **FAVOURITE PART** OF THE YEAR WAS

MY **LEAST FAVOURITE** WAS

THIS YEAR, **I LEARNED**

THIS YEAR, **I GREW**

THIS YEAR, **I TRIED**

THIS YEAR, **I VISITED**

IN 2021, **I WANT TO**

HiSTORY BUFFS

2020 FLASH BACK

200 YEARS AGO ...

Katherine Plunket was born in Co. Louth – she would live to be 111 years old!

DOES ANYONE ELSE SMELL SMOKE?

25 YEARS AGO ...

Sony releases the first PlayStation games console in Europe.

100 YEARS AGO ...

The first hair dryer went on sale. No more bad hair days!

250 YEARS AGO ...

Lexell's comet passed by Earth – the closest pass of any comet in recorded history. But don't worry, it was still 2,200,000 km away!

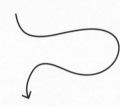

50 YEARS AGO ...

Dana wins the Eurovision for the first time for Ireland.

Can you solve this Ancient Sumerian riddle that was found on a 4000-year-old clay tablet?
Hint: You mightn't like the answer...

Q: THERE IS A HOUSE. ONE ENTERS IT BLIND AND COMES OUT SEEING. WHAT IS IT?

A: A SCHOOL.

2

MYSTERY IN MEATH

In 2003, a man was found in the bog in Co. Meath. He had been murdered. But there was one problem ... the crime happened 2,300 years ago! Can you help solve it by drawing a poster?

★ ★ ★ ★ ★

— HAVE YOU SEEN THIS MAN? —

NAME: Clonycavan Man
HEIGHT: 5' 2" **AGE:** Early 20s
DESCRIPTION: Squashed nose, crooked teeth, goatee, moustache. Hair styled with plant oils from Europe
CAUSE OF DEATH: An axe to the head

Gardaí have asked anyone who saw anything suspicious around 2,300 years ago to come forward ... slowly!

OGHAM—GEE!

The ancient Irish people used an alphabet called Ogham to write things down. Back then, they didn't have paper, so they had to carve it into rock.

Can you write your name in Ogham? **Hint:** The ancient Irish didn't use the same letters that we use today. So you might have to improvise!

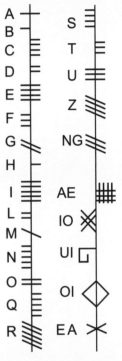

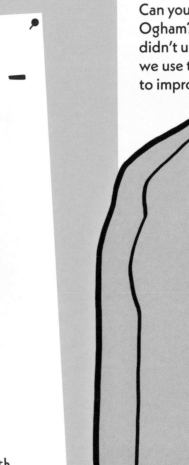

A		S	
B		T	
C		U	
D		Z	
E		NG	
F			
G		AE	
H		IO	
I		UI	
L		OI	
M			
N			
O		EA	
Q			
R			

SMARTY PANTS!

Vikings didn't actually wear helmets with horns on them. Historians think that artists made them up. Which is probably for the best, as they'd have got caught in everything!

JOKES AND RIDDLES

Try out these brainteasers on your friends and watch them scratch their heads!

HOW DO IRISH PEOPLE LIKE THEIR POTATOES?

Mash é do thoil é.

WHAT DO YOU CALL A JEDI GAA PLAYER?

Obi Wan Camogie.

WHAT'S THE FASTEST TOWN IN IRELAND?

Tuuuaaammm.

Ag gáire as Gaeilge

WHAT'S THE COLDEST TOWN IN IRELAND?

Birr.

SOMEONE JUST TOLD ME THE IRISH WORD FOR SEVEN.

I was shocked!

WHAT WAS THE IRISH VEGETARIAN RESTAURANT CALLED?

Slán go feoil.

HOW MANY PEOPLE CAN FIT IN A FIRE ENGINE?

Naonúr naonúr naonúr.

WHY DID THE STUDENT NOT WANT TO GO TO IRISH COLLEGE?

She heard there was a ban on tea.

WHAT DID THE HORSE SAY TO ITS SON?

Slán go foal!

RIDDLE ME THIS!

WHAT IS FULL OF HOLES BUT STILL HOLDS WATER?

A sponge.

I'M TALL WHEN I'M YOUNG AND SHORT WHEN I'M OLD. WHAT AM I?

A candle.

WHAT'S ALWAYS MOVING EVEN THOUGH IT NEVER LEAVES ITS BED?

A river.

WHAT CAN GO UP A DRAINPIPE DOWN, BUT NOT DOWN A DRAINPIPE UP?

An umbrella.

WHAT DO YOU THROW OUT WHEN YOU WANT TO USE IT, BUT TAKE IN WHEN YOU DON'T WANT TO USE IT?

An anchor.

WHAT QUESTION CAN YOU NEVER ANSWER YES TO?

Are you asleep yet?

WHAT IS AT THE BEGINNING OF ETERNITY, AND THE END OF TIME AND SPACE?

The letter E.

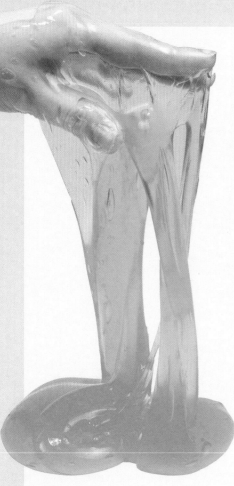

SCiENCE LAB

Feeling a bit **inventive**? Curious about how the world works? Or do you just feel like making a big mess?

SLLLLiﬂiiMMMMEEE

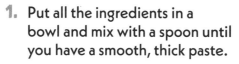

HELP! There's a worldwide **SLIME SHORTAGE**. Aliens' armpits are bone dry. Unicorns aren't pooping. Trolls have run out of snot.

Can you **WHIP UP SOME MORE SLIME** with this easy, eco-friendly **RECIPE**?

200g cornflour

50g icing sugar

175ml coconut milk

3 drops of food colouring

1. Put all the ingredients in a bowl and mix with a spoon until you have a smooth, thick paste.

2. If it's too crumbly, add another tablespoon of coconut milk. If it's too soft, add another tablespoon of cornflour.

3. The slime can dry out a little as you play with it. If this happens, just knead it with wet hands to soften it up again.

4. The best thing about this slime is that it's safe and won't stick around for a hundred years like other plastic sludge. Now you can slime to your heart's content!

Tips: Use green food colouring for alien sweat, blue for troll snot and red for dragon blood. Use glitter for unicorn poop!

SMARTY PANTS!

Laboratories can be dangerous places. The famous scientist Marie Curie studied dangerously radioactive materials. She even kept one by her bed as a nightlight!

GERM WARFARE

BACTERIA are all around us. Some are **NICE** and some **ARE NOT SO NICE!**

Scientists use **PETRI DISHES** to grow and learn about bacteria in their labs. You can **MAKE YOUR OWN** at home with the help of an adult.

1 x 12g packet of gelatine powder

1 stock cube

2 teaspoons sugar

200ml water

three containers with clear lids

tape

marker

cotton buds

1. With an adult, heat the water and add the gelatine, stock cube and sugar. Stir the mixture until it all dissolves. This is the food for the bacteria.

2. While the mixture is still hot, divide it into three and pour into the containers. Quickly put the lids on to avoid contamination.

3. Store the containers in the fridge for about four hours and remove once solid.

4. Write 'control' on one container and seal it with tape. This is so you know what happens when you do nothing. A very important part of science!

5. For the second, gently press your finger against the jelly. Close and seal the container with tape, then write your name on it.

6. For the third container, use a cotton bud to swab somewhere in your house. Try a doorknob! Now gently rub the swab on the jelly. Close and seal it, then write the location on it.

7. Leave the containers near a radiator for a few days to see what grows.

Tip: Don't try to open the containers – just look through the lids. Make sure to throw them away when you're finished.

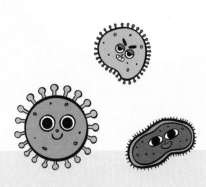

WILD AT HEART

In the summer, you can find many beautiful butterflies in the garden, flying from flower to flower.

The **peacock butterfly** has large 'eyes' on its wings to scare away predators. Try **colouring** this one in yourself.

On the hunt

Can you match these animals to their pawprints? Keep an eye out for these tracks the next time you go for a walk. If you see one in particular, **YOU'D BETTER RUN!**

BADGER

HEDGEHOG

SQUIRREL

FOX

HARE

OTTER

MOUSE

DEER

HORSE

SHEEP

DUCK

ELEPHANT

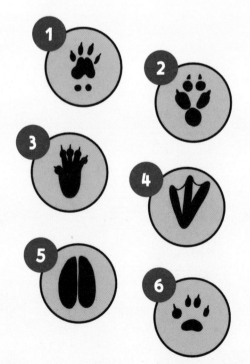

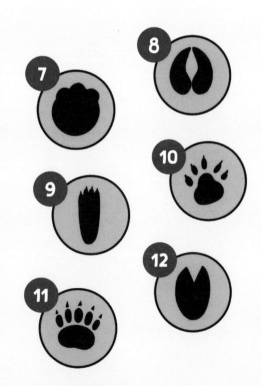

BiRD BiSCUiTS

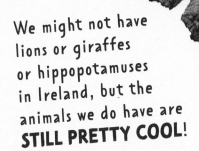

YOU WILL NEED:

250 g birdseed (or mixed nuts and seeds)
150 ml hot water
1 x 12g packet of gelatine powder
biscuit cutters or moulds
baking parchment
a knife
some string

1. Mix together the gelatine with the hot water and stir until dissolved.

2. Add the birdseed into the gelatine mixture and mix. Set aside for a few minutes.

3. Lay your moulds out on baking parchment and fill with the birdseed mixture. Press down until they're nice and full.

4. With a knife, make a small hole for your string at the top of the mixture.

5. Leave the moulds in the fridge overnight to set.

6. Pop the feeders out of the moulds, run the string through the hole, and hang them somewhere the birds can reach.

We might not have lions or giraffes or hippopotamuses in Ireland, but the animals we do have are **STILL PRETTY COOL!**

What's your **FAVOURITE ANIMAL**, and why?

_____

_____

SMARTY PANTS!

The Irish Elk was one of the biggest animals to ever live. It was about 2 metres tall at the shoulders, weighed 700 kg, and its antlers could grow to be 3.5 metres across. Good thing it died out 8,000 years ago!

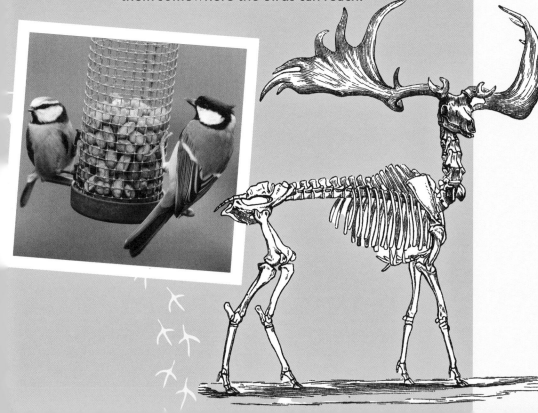

ST PATRICK'S DAY

On St Patrick's Day, everyone around the world is a little bit Irish. People throw parties, organise parades, and some cities even dye their rivers green.

NEWS TO ME

This year, parades around the country were cancelled as people stayed indoors to keep themselves safe. But that doesn't mean you can't imagine a parade of your own! Become a journalist and fill in this news report.

ST PATRICK'S DAY PARADE 2020

BY _____

This year's Saint Patrick's Day parade in _____ was full of excitement. First, there was an upside-down display of _____ from the locals. The next float was filled with colourful _____ who performed a _____. Then, ten _____ drove by, but one broke down because of _____. A marching band dressed up as _____ threw sweets out to the crowd. Unfortunately, a _____ then got loose and caused some trouble. Mrs O'Casey of New Street said: 'It was a disgrace! The music was so loud I dropped my _____!'

All in all, everyone had an interesting day and we look forward to next year's parade.

SHAMROCK SHAKES

Here's a tasty milkshake that you can make to celebrate Saint Patrick's Day (or any day you feel a little bit Irish). The green colour comes from healthy broccoli, spinach and kale ... only joking! This milkshake is made with yummy mint ice cream.

SERVES 1
2 scoops mint ice cream
200 ml milk
green food colouring (optional)
mint leaves (optional)

1. Put the ice cream and milk together in a blender and whizz them up.

2. If you want the milkshake to be extra green, you can add 1 drop of green food colouring.

3. Pour your milkshake into a tall glass. To make it look fancy, add a bunch of mint leaves on top and enjoy!

HAT'S INCREDIBLE!

This leprechaun is bored of his hat. Tophats with buckles are **soooo** last century. Can you design a new, modern hat for him?

SMARTY PANTS!

St Patrick is said to have banished the snakes from Ireland. But scientists say that there never were any snakes here to banish!

GAGA FOR GAA

spot the difference

IT WAS A STRANGE YEAR IN 2020 FOR GAA DUE TO COVID-19, BUT YOU CAN DO THESE ACTIVITIES IN YOUR OWN HOME!

Can you **spot the difference** between these two football scenes? There are **six** in total.

GIVE IT A HURL

Try this drill at home to keep your swing in tip-top shape.

1

Stand 3 metres back from a wall with a hurl and sliotar.

2

Strike the ball off the wall as many times as possible in 60 seconds, controlling the sliotar on the way back. Watch out for windows!

3

Do it first on your left side and then repeat on your right. Try to beat your score tomorrow.

BEAT THE GOALIE

It's extra time at the All-Ireland Senior Football Championship finals. Can you make it past the opposite team to score a goal?

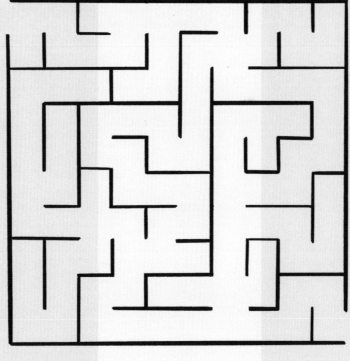

OPPOSITES ATTRACT

This exercise is great for improving your handball skills. You'll need a partner or parent for this one.

1. One person will be the catcher and the other the thrower.

2. Stand 2 metres apart from each other.

3. The thrower calls 'left' or 'right' as they throw the ball.

4. The catcher must catch the ball with the OPPOSITE hand to whatever is called!

SMARTY PANTS!

In the story of the 'Táin Bó Cuailgne', a young Irish warrior called Setanta used a hurl and sliotar to kill a guard dog. The owner of the dog, Culann, was angry, so the boy agreed to act as a guard dog in his place. The boy became known as Cú Chulainn, or Culann's hound.

WRITER'S ROOM
CHATTING WITH JASON BYRNE

Do you want to visit the moon, fight crime, discover magical creatures or meet your hero? You can do it from your bedroom – **just write it down!**

Q. DID YOU ALWAYS WANT TO BE AN AUTHOR?

A. Funnily enough, I never wanted to be a 'Jason' – I wanted to be an 'Arthur', so that when I grew up, I would be called 'Arthur the Author'.

Q. HOW DID YOU COME UP WITH THE IDEA FOR *THE ACCIDENTAL ADVENTURES OF ONION O'BRIEN*?

A. I was on an accidental adventure in Tibet at the beach (I was the first person in the world to be at the beach in Tibet). While I had my toes in the water, an onion floated in from the sea. I picked it up, looked out to the Tibetan Sea, and watched a boat sail by called *The O'Brien*. I looked at the boat, then at the onion, and ... hey presto!

Q. WHAT TIPS DO YOU HAVE FOR YOUNG WRITERS?

A. Make sure you have good characters before you even start. The story will then write itself, as the characters will tell you what they want to do. Onion is always telling me what he likes – I just listen to him and type.

Q. TELL US A JOKE!

A. What did the left eye say to the right eye?

BETWEEN US, SOMETHING SMELLS. (That's Onion O'Brien's favourite joke, he just told me.)

THE WRITE WAY

HERE'S AN EXAMPLE:

HAMMOCK
WATERMELON
GIRAFFE
CRUSTY

Open your favourite book on a random page and pick a word. Do this three more times. You're going to write a story that includes the four words you chose!

One day, I woke up in a **HAMMOCK**. This was odd, because I had gone to sleep in my own bedroom.

All around me ... I could hear strange voices jabbering. I looked down to see six robot **GIRAFFES** staring at me. One of them was eating a fruit salad, and they all looked very surprised.

Suddenly ... a **CRUSTY** old giraffe cleared his throat and told me that I had taken a wrong turn. The room went dark.

The next thing I knew ... I opened my eyes and I was back in my own room. But I had a slice of **WATERMELON** in my hand.

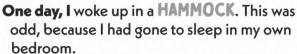 **YOUR TURN!**

One day, I ...

All around me ...

Suddenly ...

The next thing I knew ...

OUT AND ABOUT
Go explore!

The **HIGHEST MOUNTAIN** in Ireland is ...

The **SMALLEST COUNTY** in Ireland is ...

The **BIGGEST LAKE** in Ireland is ...

The county with the **SHORTEST COASTLINE** in Ireland is ...

The **BIGGEST PARK** in Ireland is ...

The **LONGEST RIVER** in Ireland is ...

FLOWER POWER

PRESSING FLOWERS IS AN EASY WAY TO KEEP THEM BRIGHT AND FRESH FOR YEARS.

1. Pick some flowers and **gently dry them** with kitchen paper. Try to get a nice mix of colours.

2. Place the flowers face down on a sheet of paper. Cover them with another sheet of paper and **gently press down**.

3. Place the two sheets of paper under some books – they'll need to be heavy, so **pick some big ones!**

4. Leave the flowers to press for **about three weeks**.

5. Remove the books, and gently **peel off the top sheet of paper**.

6. **Tada!** You should have some beautifully pressed flowers.

TIP: You can use your pressed flowers to decorate notebooks, birthday cards or bookmarks.

WE LIVE IN ONE OF THE MOST BEAUTIFUL PLACES IN THE WORLD, AND THERE'S PLENTY TO SEE AND DO.

Colour in the counties that you've visited.

While you're at it, can you name the emoji landmarks?

1

2

3

4

5

6

7

8

9

10

SMARTY PANTS!

The longest place name in Ireland is Muckanaghederdauhaulia. It translates to 'piggery between two brines'.

CRISPY BUSINESS

THE STORY OF TAYTO

In 1954, Joe 'Spud' Murphy had an idea. Back then, all crisps were unflavoured, except for a small bag of salt that came in each bag.

He decided to call his company **Tayto**, after the way his son pronounced the word 'potato'. **The crisps were a great success!**

Joe Murphy came up with a way to flavour the crisps as they were made. His first flavour was **cheese and onion**, and he soon began to try new ones, like **salt and vinegar** and **prawn cocktail**.

Are **YOU** the next **SPUD MURPHY**? Could you come up with **AN INVENTION** that would take the food world by storm?

Draw your idea here!

First, think of a problem:

COLD BUTTER IS TOO HARD TO SPREAD ON SOFT BREAD.

Now, think of a solution:

A KNIFE THAT CAN HEAT ITSELF UP!

HOW CRISPS ARE MADE

We Irish love our crisps. We eat about **1.3 MILLION** packets of them a day!

YAY!

1 Farmers harvest potatoes from their fields and deliver them to a factory.

2 The potatoes are checked to make sure they're the right size – small ones are removed and bigger ones are cut up.

3 The potatoes are cut into thin slices by a machine.

4 The slices are fried in hot vegetable oil to make them nice and crispy.

5 Flavourings are added at the end to make the crisps tastier.

6 The crisps are packaged and sent out to shops all around the country.

When Fred Baur died in 2008, his ashes were put into a Pringles container and buried. Sound strange? Well, he invented the can!

SMARTY PANTS!

TECH CORNER

Video games, computers, robots, coding and AI – read all about it! But the photographer is on their holidays. **Can you fill in for them by drawing pictures to go with these articles?**

TECHNOLOGY TIMES

ROBOT CHEFS

A team of engineers have trained a robot to prepare an omelette, all the way from cracking the eggs to serving up the finished dish. Bon appetit!

FIVE IS LIVE

In 2020, Sony announced the PlayStation 5, its next-generation gaming console. It will have updated software, brand new games, and a cool new look. But it'll be pricey – better start doing extra chores now!

LISTEN TO MUMMY

Scientists used scans to map the vocal cords of an ancient Egyptian priest named Nesyamun who lived about 3,000 years ago. When hooked up to a voice box in the lab, a 3-D printed mould of the mummy's vocal cords made a noise – it sounded like 'Eeeehhh'. Guess he wasn't too impressed!

BUILDER'S BUM

Scientists have suggested that astronauts might be able to make cement from their own pee. Urea, an ingredient of urine, was mixed with replica moon dust to make a tough cement that could be used for building.

FROM ZERO TO HERO

Binary code is how computers talk and represent information, using only two digits: **0** and **1**.

Letters, numbers, pictures – everything you see on a computer screen is made up of **different combinations of these two numbers.**

Programmers say that binary code is as easy as **01, 10, 11!**

CAN YOU WRITE YOUR NAME?

WORD SCRAMBLE

These computing words have gotten all mixed up. Can you unscramble them?

nitomro

sgmea

docgin

rosposcer

adat

remmyo

rawrehda

magerpromar

kronetw

paplot

losenoc

ASCII CODE: CHARACTER TO BINARY

A	01000001	**N**	01001110
B	01000010	**O**	01001111
C	01000011	**P**	01010000
D	01000100	**Q**	01010001
E	01000101	**R**	01010010
F	01000110	**S**	01010011
G	01000111	**T**	01010100
H	01001000	**U**	01010101
I	01001001	**V**	01010110
J	01001010	**W**	01010111
K	01001011	**X**	01011000
L	01001100	**Y**	01011001
M	01001101	**Z**	01011010

ON THE FARM
HOMEWARD BOUND

On an Irish farm, you will find many different types of animal. Can you get each one back to its pen?

Oops.

Were you supposed to get rid of those old potatoes? Now they're **SPROUTING LIKE ALIENS**. Don't throw them out yet – you can use them to **GROW A FRESH BATCH!**

The best time of year for this is **EARLY SPRING**. You can do this in your garden or in a pot. Simply bury the potato about 10 cm deep into the soil, with the 'eyes' facing up.

Add more soil on top as the plant grows. After the plant flowers, the potatoes are **READY FOR HARVESTING**.

IN IRELAND, WE'RE LUCKY TO HAVE ACCESS TO LOTS OF FRESH FOOD THAT COMES TO US FROM IRISH FARMERS. SO EAT UP!

N	R	Q	P	V	C	T	H	L	F	C	V	S	N	N
G	D	O	H	A	S	R	I	K	E	E	Y	I	M	E
W	K	S	T	E	H	V	L	A	R	B	Q	L	G	K
F	A	T	V	C	E	K	C	A	T	S	Y	A	H	C
Q	L	R	W	S	A	U	F	M	I	S	M	G	S	I
E	A	G	T	H	O	R	H	L	L	F	P	E	L	H
H	Z	O	T	K	K	M	T	I	I	B	E	O	M	C
O	C	P	A	S	T	U	R	E	S	W	L	D	R	S
K	R	E	F	I	E	H	V	Z	E	D	D	O	B	C
M	S	C	E	J	C	Y	N	X	R	U	K	C	X	Y
O	X	E	H	G	O	R	O	L	U	A	B	K	Y	Z
G	A	X	W	A	O	I	L	Q	W	E	V	Y	Q	D
Q	Y	W	X	X	R	A	P	R	F	D	U	R	X	F
F	R	K	O	Z	L	D	C	N	C	Y	C	I	O	L
J	R	G	E	W	H	N	H	B	E	S	U	W	G	B

TRACTOR SILAGE **CATTLE**

CHICKEN **FERTILISER** CROPS

HARVEST PASTURE **DAIRY**

HEIFER **EWE** ORCHARD

LIVESTOCK HAYSTACK

WHAT DO YOU CALL A SLEEPING COW?

A bull-dozer!

WHAT DO YOU CALL A BIRD THAT'S AFRAID TO FLY?

Chicken.

zZZ

WHY DID THE SCARECROW WIN AN AWARD?

He was outstanding in his field!

CLIMATE CRISIS

Climate change is definitely not cool! Roll the dice to get some ideas to help create a greener world.

You'll need a **dice** and something to represent your player, like a **coin or a small stone**.

WACKY WEATHER

RECORD-BREAKERS

Met Éireann keeps track of all the weather in Ireland so that they can better understand our climate.

Of course, their records don't go back forever – **the last Ice Age must have been pretty chilly**! But since they've been keeping an eye on our country, we've had some **pretty interesting weather**.

The **HOTTEST** day ever was 33.3°C in Kilkenny in 1887

The **COLDEST** day ever was -19.1°C in Sligo in 1881

The **WETTEST** day ever was 243.5mm of rain in Kerry in 1993

The **STRONGEST** gust ever was 182km/h in Limerick in 1945

FORECAST IT

Weather forecasters use different **symbols** to describe what the weather looks like.

Can you look outside your window and **make your own**?

Try doing one for every day of the week and see if you can get it right!

Weather	Symbol	Wind Speed (mph)	Symbol	Cloud Cover (%)	Symbol
DRIZZLE	🪶	1–4		0	○
FOG	≡	5–8		10	◐
HAIL	△	9–14		20–30	◔
HAZE	∞	15–20			
RAIN	●	21–25		40	◑
SHOWER	▽	26–31		50	◐
SLEET	◬	32–37			
SMOKE	∿	38–43		60	⊖
SNOW	✳	44–49		70–80	◕
THUNDERSTORM	⚡	50–54		90	◑
HURRICANE	🌀	55–60		100	●
		61–66			
		67–71			
		72–77			

MONDAY	TUESDAY	WEDNESDAY	THURSDAY	FRIDAY	SATURDAY	SUNDAY

IN IRELAND, THEY SAY IF YOU CAN'T SEE THE MOUNTAINS, IT'S RAINING. IF YOU CAN SEE THEM, IT'S ABOUT TO RAIN!

CLOUD

HURRICANE

SHOWER

BLIZZARD

TEMPERATURE

FREEZE

CELSIUS

FLOOD

FOGGY

THUNDER

LIGHTNING

RAINBOW

SLEET

STORM

X	W	Y	E	I	Z	H	P	S	N	W	J	E	Q	E
E	A	W	R	M	P	R	T	C	D	I	N	D	K	Z
Q	A	D	U	P	R	O	E	J	V	A	D	O	V	E
W	C	P	T	T	R	E	L	W	C	U	M	N	W	E
N	E	Z	A	M	X	E	K	I	O	C	N	P	T	R
S	L	P	R	U	C	O	R	L	I	H	J	A	B	F
L	S	J	E	X	B	R	C	R	F	T	S	Q	A	T
E	I	E	P	F	U	L	I	G	H	T	N	I	N	G
E	U	M	M	H	O	J	I	U	F	L	O	O	D	L
T	S	G	E	Z	D	G	N	Z	K	S	V	X	I	M
I	L	G	T	L	N	D	G	X	Z	Y	J	Y	J	O
Y	G	L	K	F	E	G	K	Y	F	A	B	C	C	N
Z	Y	T	F	R	W	O	B	N	I	A	R	J	R	I
N	P	U	S	C	T	X	X	L	L	Z	H	D	M	W
J	O	P	A	Q	O	O	O	X	L	D	I	J	G	P

SMARTY PANTS!

Every year, Met Éireann works with other weather forecasters across Europe to come up with a list of names for winter storms. But they also ask the public to send in suggestions, so you could try naming one after your annoying brother or sister!

27

PARTY PEOPLE
FREAKY FESTIVALS

In **2020**, many festivals around Ireland were cancelled due to COVID-19. But we can still look forward to next year!

POC FADA translates to long puck, which is exactly what this event is about. Competitors gather at Annaverna Mountain to finish a course in as few pucks as possible.

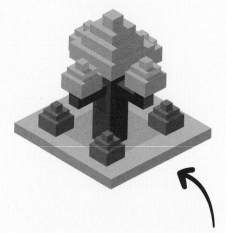

Every year, **MINEVENTION** celebrates all things Minecraft! They celebrate the game through challenges, tournaments, costume contests and Q&As with famous YouTubers.

THE IRISH BOG SNORKELLING CHAMPIONSHIPS are exactly what they sound like! In Co. Monaghan, brave snorkellers must swim through the bog and try to get the fastest time.

Can you design a crown fit for a goat king?

PUCK FAIR takes place in Co. Kerry. A farmer goes up into the mountains to catch a goat to be crowned king of the fair.

NEW YEAR, NEW YOU

DIFFERENT CULTURES CELEBRATE THE NEW YEAR AT DIFFERENT TIMES, BOTH IN IRELAND AND AROUND THE WORLD.

Diwali is a festival celebrated by Hindus. People fill their homes with lights and exchange gifts to celebrate the new year and the power of light over darkness.

The **Hijri New Year** is the first day of Muharram, the first month in the Islamic calendar. Muslims make a special effort to fast, pray and think about the past year.

Chinese New Year has been celebrated for many centuries. During the festivities, people welcome the new year with ceremonies to bring good luck and happiness.

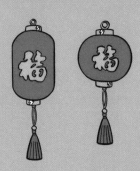

SMARTY PANTS!

2020 was the Chinese Year of the Rat. Rats are clever, quick thinkers, and a symbol of wealth.

CHINESE PAPER LANTERN

1. Start with an A4 sheet of paper. Cut a strip of paper from the long edge, about 2cm wide. This will be the handle of the lantern.

2. Fold the paper in half lengthwise. Cut strips from the folded edge towards the open edge. Be careful not to cut all the way through!

3. Unfold the paper and loop it around to form a tube. Tape the short ends of the paper together.

4. Add any decorations you like, tape on the handle you made in step 1, and you're done!

RUGBY REBELS
NEAT NICKNAMES

IRELAND WAS UNLUCKY IN THE 2020 SIX NATIONS, AND MANY RUGBY GAMES WERE POSTPONED. BUT YOU CAN STILL BE A FAN!

Can you match these Rugby Union teams with their nicknames?

TEAM NAME	NICKNAME
NEW ZEALAND	SPRINGBOKS
SOUTH AFRICA	MEN IN GREEN
ENGLAND	RED AND WHITES
WALES	BRAVE BLOSSOMS
IRELAND	DRAGONS
AUSTRALIA	ALL BLACKS
FRANCE	LOS PUMAS
ARGENTINA	GLI AZZURRI
SCOTLAND	WALLABIES
JAPAN	LES BLEUS
ITALY	BRAVEHEARTS

DIY JERSEY

CAN YOU COME UP WITH A BRAND-NEW KIT FOR YOUR TEAM?

You'll need a logo, a slogan and a sponsor.

Try for a try

Can you avoid the other players and get the ball across the line?

SMARTY PANTS!

The first rugby balls had rounder ends than the modern, oval balls ... because they were made from pig bladders!

DROPKICK   SCRUM

CONVERSION   TRY

THROW   CAUTION

RUCK   TACKLE

FLANKER   HAKA

HOOKER   KNOCK

WINGER

C	G	L	S	C	R	U	M	M	R	D	W	L	D	X
I	O	J	B	E	N	S	S	N	E	R	P	J	N	H
T	E	N	G	D	V	M	G	D	K	O	J	T	E	J
S	H	N	V	T	H	Z	H	C	O	P	W	S	P	G
E	I	R	Q	E	Q	U	A	N	O	K	Q	N	S	F
W	I	L	O	D	R	U	M	F	H	I	X	K	M	O
Y	D	U	W	W	T	S	O	A	G	C	L	N	F	D
Y	R	B	C	I	T	G	I	K	E	K	W	O	J	Z
E	Y	C	O	C	U	R	R	O	G	V	J	C	J	E
I	L	N	L	Y	Q	A	B	R	N	E	G	K	A	Z
S	G	K	J	D	R	A	J	L	B	C	Z	H	R	V
C	F	E	C	Q	A	T	R	E	K	N	A	L	F	R
T	D	A	K	A	H	N	F	Q	F	K	Q	K	U	X
N	D	Y	R	F	T	A	I	I	B	I	B	C	L	A
S	J	J	Z	B	Y	D	N	D	T	X	K	Z	P	D

KITCHEN CORNER

TAKING THE CAKE

Can you **finish off** this birthday cake? **Here** are some **icing patterns** you can copy. Make sure to use lots of different flavours and toppings!

ARE YOU A MASTER CHEF OR CAN YOU BURN A GLASS OF WATER? BON APPÉTIT ...

YUM! DELICIOUSLY TRUE OR TASTELESSLY FALSE?

1. Honey never, ever goes off. _____

2. Fruit salad trees don't actually exist. _____

3. Pineapples take two to three months to grow. _____

4. Lemons float but limes sink. _____

5. White chocolate isn't actually chocolate. _____

6. Every banana you eat is a clone. _____

7. Cheese is the most stolen food in the world. _____

8. On *Sesame Street*, the Cookie Monster eats real cookies. _____

9. Roman soldiers used to be paid in sugar. _____

10. Arachibutyrophobia is the fear of getting peanut butter stuck to the roof of your mouth. _____

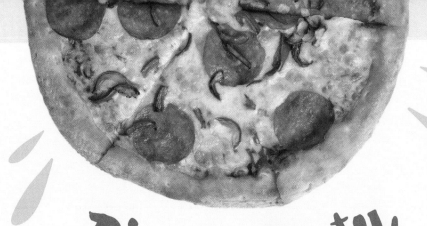

Pizza Party

MAKES 4 PIZZA BASES

7g dried yeast sachet

½ teaspoon sugar

2 tablespoons olive oil

250ml warm water

500g strong white flour

1 tablespoon salt

Toppings: Tomato sauce, cheese, vegetables, meat – anything you like!

1. In a jug, mix the yeast, sugar and oil into the warm water and leave for a few minutes until you see bubbles.

2. Put the flour and salt into a big bowl and make a well in the middle. Pour in the yeasty water.

3. Using a fork, start swirling the flour into the liquid. Then use your (clean!) hands to knead until you have a smooth, springy dough.

4. Put the dough in a big floury bowl and cover with a damp cloth. Leave to rise in a warm room for at least an hour.

5. While the dough is rising, heat your oven to 220°C and start getting your favourite toppings ready.

6. Divide the dough up into four little balls. Use a rolling pin to flatten them into bases.

7. Put the bases on a baking tray, then add your tomato sauce and toppings. Bake for 15 minutes until nice and crispy. Enjoy!

SMARTY PANTS!

The Hawaiian pizza was invented in 1962 by a man from Greece who ran a pizza place in Canada. Not everyone's a fan – the president of Iceland told schoolchildren he would ban pineapple on pizza if he had the power.

YUM!

CRAIC AGUS CEOL

CONNECT THE DOTS TO KEEP THE SEISIÚN GOING!

SMARTY PANTS!

The Fleadh Cheoil is the world's largest annual celebration of Irish music, language, song and dance. Sadly, it was cancelled in 2020, but 2021 will be bigger and better than ever!

DANCING SHOES

IRELAND IS FAMOUS AROUND THE WORLD FOR ITS DANCE, MUSIC, AND SENSE OF FUN.

Irish dancing can be done in a group or solo. Two common types of Irish dance are the jig and the reel. But how can you tell the difference?

If you can say 'rashers and sausages, rashers and sausages' in time to the music it's a **JIG**.

If you can say 'double decker, double decker' in time to the music it's a **REEL**.

Now, try listening to some Irish music and see if you can tell what it is!

ALL SHOOK UP

Can you **unscramble** the names of these **Irish musical artists**?

noob

tomrde nekdeyn

zirohe

linal ronah

eth ripsct

fieswelt

citrepu stih

DAY AT THE ZOO

Dublin Zoo is one of the oldest zoos in the world, having opened in 1831. It's an amazing place to visit. You'll find all sorts of animals there, along with zookeepers who are working to protect wildlife for generations to come.

A ZOOKEEPER'S DIARY

The **keepers** at Dublin Zoo devote their lives to the welfare and care of animals and to understanding their needs. They know all about the natural habitat of the animals, their diet and behaviours.

They're also very passionate about **conservation**, which means working to protect animals all over the world to make sure they don't become endangered or, even worse, extinct.

DEAR DIARY,

What a day! A new animal arrived at Dublin Zoo, unlike anything I've ever seen before.

It has _____ ears, a huge _____, and _____ legs.

Instead of toes, it has _____ and its tail looks like _____.

It is covered in _____ and when you touch it, it feels like a _____.

It makes a noise like a _____ playing a _____.

And the smell! If you mixed _____ and _____ you'd know what it smelled like.

I don't know where we're going to put it. It's too _____ for the giraffes and too _____ for the flamingos.

EEK!

ACROSS

2. I'm a real hairy howler.

7. I'm often in a hump, maybe in two.

8. My eyes are no good but my ears help me soar.

9. I'm a bit spiky, but I'm looking for grub.

10. I'm a big fan of bamboo.

11. I have bumpy skin and I pretend to cry.

13. I'm tall and have a purple tongue.

14. I throw a good punch, but I've a baby on board.

16. I sound like dessert but have a nasty sting.

DOWN

1. People used to think my cry was the banshee.

3. I wear pink feathers and have very long legs.

4. Humans borrowed my pattern to cross the road.

5. I never change my spots.

6. I'm the fastest animal in the world.

12. My heart is the size of a car.

15. At night, you'll hear me asking Who? Who?

In 2013, a zoo in the UK put a temporary ban on visitors wearing animal prints so their animals wouldn't get confused.

SMARTY PANTS!

GOING VIRAL

INTERVIEW WITH SUPER SCIENTIST
~~~
PROFESSOR LUKE O'NEILL

In 2020, a **global pandemic** spread around the world.

For a time, **COVID-19** changed the way we lived, worked and played.

But the whole country came together to **fight the virus**.

Hi Professor O'Neill,

Scientists around the world have been working hard to understand the new coronavirus that spread around the world in 2020. Could you tell us a bit about it?

WHAT IS COVID-19?

COVID-19 is a disease caused by a nasty virus called SARS-CoV2. Viruses are tiny creatures – 50 million of them would fit on the full stop at the end of this sentence. Millions of people around the world have been infected. The vast majority of people fight the virus with their immune systems, and are well. A small number get very sick, and sadly some die.

HOW DOES IT SPREAD?

Because the virus lives in our lungs and throat, it is spread when we speak, shout or cough. It comes out in tiny droplets, which can land on surfaces like tabletops. The virus can get onto your hands, and you might infect yourself or spread it onto other surfaces. If someone who is infected is speaking or coughing near you, the virus can get into your mouth or nose or even your eyes.

WHAT HAPPENS NEXT?

The virus is slowly dying out because anyone who has had it has killed it with their immune systems. It might come back, though, as many countries still have a lot of infected people. Science will save us from this virus, either through medicines to give to sick people or by inventing a vaccine, which will stop us getting infected in the first place!

BEAT THE BUG

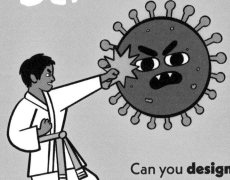

Can you **design a poster** to help people remember how to **stay safe**? Make sure you include **Professor Luke O'Neill's advice**!

WHAT CAN WE DO TO PROTECT OURSELVES AND OTHERS?

We need to keep away from others – this is called social distancing. Two metres is fine as any droplets will fall to the ground or get blown away. We also need to wash our hands a lot in case we have any of the virus on them, and we need to wear a mask, as that will stop us spreading it to others.

HOW TO PREVENT COVID-19

AROUND THE WORLD

How's your **GEOGRAPHY**? Are you a globetrotter in training or do you get lost going to the shop?

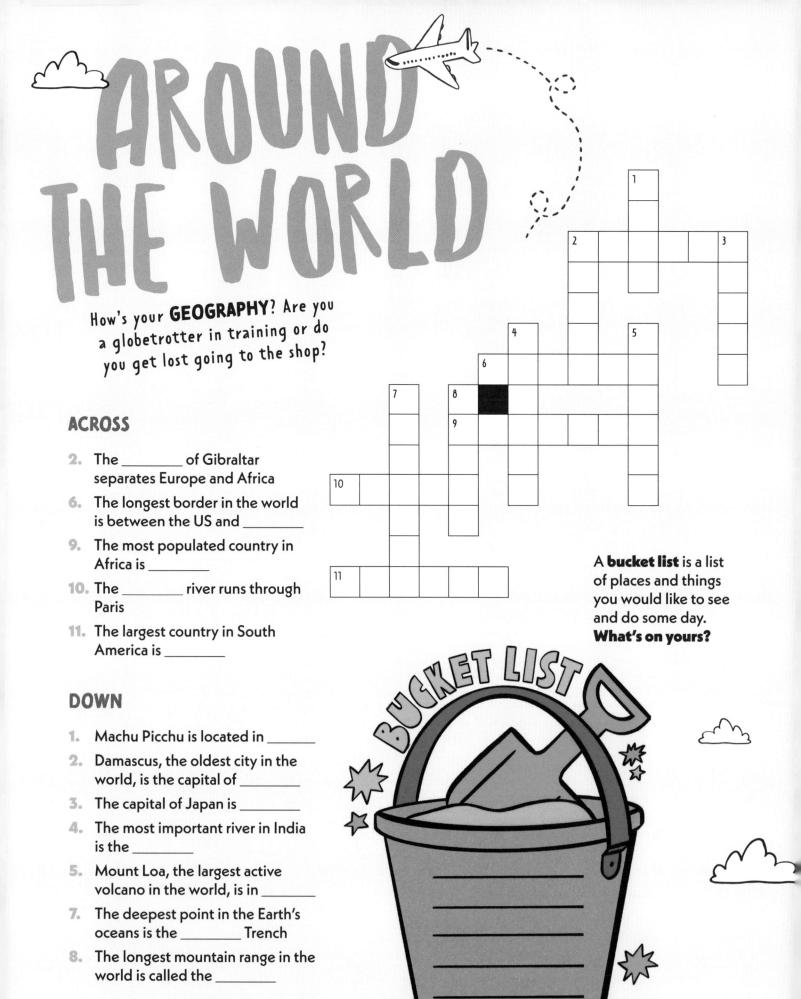

ACROSS

2. The _____ of Gibraltar separates Europe and Africa
6. The longest border in the world is between the US and _____
9. The most populated country in Africa is _____
10. The _____ river runs through Paris
11. The largest country in South America is _____

DOWN

1. Machu Picchu is located in _____
2. Damascus, the oldest city in the world, is the capital of _____
3. The capital of Japan is _____
4. The most important river in India is the _____
5. Mount Loa, the largest active volcano in the world, is in _____
7. The deepest point in the Earth's oceans is the _____ Trench
8. The longest mountain range in the world is called the _____

A **bucket list** is a list of places and things you would like to see and do some day. **What's on yours?**

BUCKET LIST

MAP iT OUT

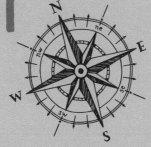

Congratulations! You've been elected **President for Life** of your **own country**. Tell us a little bit about it.

HAIRYBUTTELAND

WILD CARNIBEASTS

My **COUNTRY'S NAME** is

We **ARE FAMOUS** for

Our **NATIONAL FOOD** is

Our **FAVOURITE SPORT** is

WILD CARNIBEAST TOENAILS

UPSIDE-DOWN CURLING

Now you just need to **draw a map** to help visitors to get around. Add in rivers, forests, mountains, deserts, cities and wild animals – **use your imagination!**

SMARTY PANTS!

Mapmakers used to put fake towns and islands on their maps. That way, if they saw the same place on another map, they would know it was a copy!

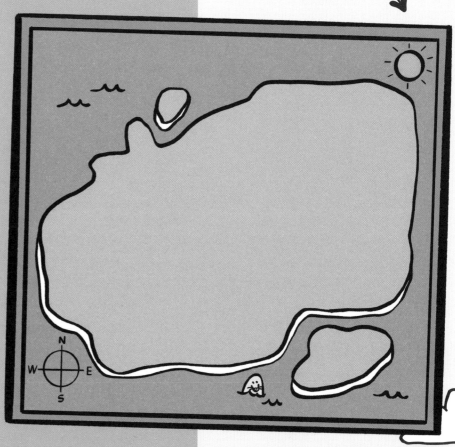

HERO OR VILLAIN?

BECOME A SUPERHERO

TIME TO SAVE THE WORLD!

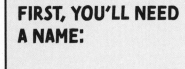

FIRST, YOU'LL NEED A NAME:

_____

I AM ... THE AMAZING STEEL FOX

I AM ... THE GOLDEN WONDER

NEXT, YOU'LL NEED A SUPERPOWER:

_____

_____

I CAN MAKE COPIES OF MYSELF TO FOOL MY ENEMIES.

I CAN ALWAYS TELL WHO FARTED.

YOU'LL ALSO NEED A BACKSTORY:

_____

_____

I WAS KIDNAPPED BY ALIENS WHO TAUGHT ME TO DANCE.

I WAS RAISED IN THE FOREST – I'M HALF-MAN, HALF-HEDGEHOG.

NOW, YOU'LL NEED HEADQUARTERS:

_____

_____

MY HQ IS ON TOP OF THE SPIRE IN DUBLIN.

MY HQ IS IN A COSY CAVE UNDER A CLIFF.

NOW, DRAW YOUR SUPERHERO SELF.

FINALLY, YOU'LL NEED A CAUSE:

_____

_____

MY JOB IS TO SAVE THE WORLD FROM BAD SPELLING!

I'M GOING TO BUILD AN ARMY OF CRIME-FIGHTING ROBOTS!

BECOME A SUPERVILLAIN

TIME TO DESTROY THE WORLD!

FIRST, YOU'LL NEED A NAME:

_____

I AM ... THE MYSTERIOUS MADAME X

I AM ... THE TERRIFYING TIGER KING

NEXT, YOU'LL NEED AN EVIL POWER:

_____

_____

I CAN START FIRES WITH MY MIND.

I CAN MAKE YOUR BUM ITCHY JUST BY LOOKING AT YOU.

YOU'LL ALSO NEED A BACKSTORY:

_____

_____

_____

I FELL INTO A BUCKET OF SQUIDS AND CAME OUT WITH TENTACLES.

I WAS CURSED BY A WITCH AFTER I STUCK MY TONGUE OUT AT HER.

NOW, DRAW YOUR SUPERVILLAIN SELF.

NOW, YOU'LL NEED A LAIR WHERE YOU CAN PLOT:

_____

_____

MY LAIR IS IN A SATELLITE, LOOKING DOWN ON EARTH.

MY LAIR IS UNDER YOUR BED.

FINALLY, YOU'LL NEED AN EVIL PLAN:

_____

_____

I'M GOING TO BLOW UP THE MOON TO SEE IF IT'S MADE OF CHEESE!

I'M GOING TO MAKE SURE EVERYONE HAS A BLOCKED NOSE, FOREVER!

HAUNTING HALLOWEEN

DID YOU KNOW THAT THE IRISH INVENTED HALLOWEEN?

During the ancient festival of Samhain, the Celts would light fires and wear costumes to scare away ghosts.

The people believed that this marked the end of summer and the beginning of the long, cold winter.

BAT OUT OF HELL

Make your own batty decorations with an egg carton!

1. Cut the top lid off your egg carton.

2. Now, cut down the middle so that you have three cups in a line.

3. Cut notches in the bottoms of the two outside cups to make them look like wings.

4. Paint your bat black. Once it has dried, you can add eyes and some fangs, and hang your bat from a string.

SMARTY PANTS!

These days, carving pumpkins is a tradition at Halloween. But originally, Irish people would carve scary faces on turnips to frighten their neighbours!

SPOOKY STORIES

Everybody loves scary stories. Here's an easy way to start one off. All you need is a dice, a piece of paper, and your imagination.

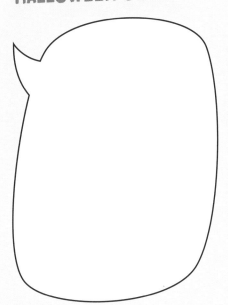

Here's how it works. You roll the dice and use the number of spots that appear to choose your character, location, setting and problem.

ONE DAY, A

WAS IN

DURING

AND DISCOVERED

For example:

ONE DAY, A **GROANING GHOST** WAS IN A **MYSTERIOUS CASTLE** DURING **A TALENT SHOW** AND DISCOVERED **A HORRIBLE MESS**.

	1ST ROLL: CHARACTER	2ND ROLL: LOCATION	3RD ROLL: SETTING	4TH ROLL: PROBLEM
⚀	Hungry zombie	A dark graveyard	A terrible storm	A sore tooth
⚁	Lonely vampire	A haunted ship	A wedding	A missing person
⚂	Groaning ghost	A mysterious castle	A birthday party	A terrifying noise
⚃	Cranky werewolf	A deep jungle	A football match	A dangerous secret
⚄	One-eyed witch	An underground cave	A talent show	A lost treasure
⚅	Annoyed monster	An abandoned hospital	A camping trip	A horrible mess

SOCCER SHOWDOWN

CAN YOU MAKE IT ALL THE WAY TO THE CUP?

You'll need a **dice** and something to represent your player, like a **coin or a small stone.**

UNTIED SHOELACE - go back 1 space

OPEN GOAL - go forward 3 spaces

BICYCLE KICK - fly forward 3 spaces

YELLOW CARD - go back 2 spaces

PENALTY - go forward 2 spaces

KICK OFF!

FLICK-ON - go forward 2 spaces

RECORD BREAKERS

2 1 3

WE MIGHT NOT BE THE TALLEST, SMARTEST, STRONGEST OR FASTEST ... BUT IRISH PEOPLE HAVE STILL BROKEN SOME PRETTY IMPRESSIVE RECORDS!

6

The **longest-serving live match commentator** is the GAA legend Mícheál Ó Muircheartaigh. He began his broadcasting career in 1949 and retired in 2010 at the age of 80.

5

Better work off that breakfast. The world's **biggest tap-dancing class** took place in Belfast in 2018. A grand total of 445 people took part! That must have been a noisy class...

1

In 2016 Poplar Linens created the world's **largest tea towel** for the Mayo Roscommon Hospice. The tea towel measures 15 metres x 10.5 metres. That will mop up a lot of spills!

4

Feeling hungry now? Butcher Barry John Crowe from Cavan achieved the title of **most sausages produced in a minute** with 78 in 2017.

2

Speaking of spills, we also hold the record for the **most cups of tea** made in one hour – and no, it wasn't your granny who set it. Lidl's team of 12 managed to make 1,848 cups in 43 minutes at the 2015 Ploughing Championships.

3

And what's tea without biscuits? Hassetts Bakery in Co. Cork holds the record for **most cookies baked in an hour**. They made a total of 4,695 cookies, all in aid of raising money for the Irish Cancer Society.

7

He just missed the **largest gathering of people dressed as sumo wrestlers**, by Purple House Cancer Support in Co. Wicklow in 2015. An amazing 293 people took part!

8

From putting clothes on to taking them off – the **fastest time to shear a sheep** is 37.90 seconds, set by Ivan Scott in Castlepollard, Co. Westmeath, in 2010. Not baaaad!

9

Staying in the animal kingdom, Dingle's most famous resident is the **longest-lived solitary dolphin**. Fungie was first sighted off the coast of Kerry in 1983. He is estimated to be at least 40 years old.

10

And finally ... **the largest gathering of people dressed as leprechauns** was achieved by 1,263 people in Bandon on St Patrick's Day 2012.

DO TRY THIS AT HOME!

Here's some records you can try to beat yourself:

Most Smarties eaten in 1 minute blindfolded using chopsticks

Record to beat	Your record
20	—

Largest bubblegum bubble blown

Record to beat	Your record
51 cm	—

Most spoons balanced on the body

Record to beat	Your record
79	—

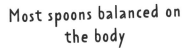

Most football touches in 30 seconds keeping the ball in the air

Record to beat	Your record
252	—

Most socks put on one foot in 30 seconds

Record to beat	Your record
28	—

CROKE PARK

Are you mad for GAA?
Let's see how much you know about this famous stadium.

TRUE OR FALSE?

1.
Croke Park was named after a frog scientist, Thomas Croak.

2.
Staff at Croke Park use hunting birds to keep seagulls away.

3. ✗
The first ever soccer match was played in Croke Park in 2007.

4.
The famous boxer Muhammad Ali fought in Croke Park in 1972.

5.
In 1939, the all-Ireland Hurling Final took place on such a beautiful day that they called it the Sunshine and Rainbows Final.

6. ✗
The GAA bought the stadium for £3,500 in 1913.

7.
The pitch at Croke Park is about the same size as a soccer pitch.

8.
Outside Ireland, there are about 40 GAA clubs around the world.

9.
The Sam Maguire and Liam MacCarthy cups presented to the winning teams are replicas.

10.
The top of Croke Park is nearly 10 storeys high.

A-MAZE-ING SEATS

You've gotten front-row seats to the **All-Ireland Final**, and you've just picked up some chips and a soft drink. **Quick!** The game is about to start and you need to get to your seat.

GOING CLUBBING

In the GAA Museum at Croke Park, the Club Wall shows off the **crests of every GAA club** in Ireland and around the world.

Can you **design a new one**? You'll need some images, a name and a motto.

HERE ARE SOME EXAMPLES TO GET YOU STARTED.

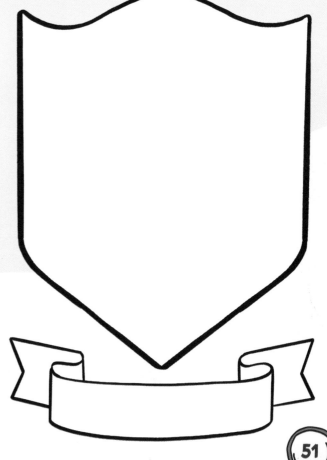

TOY SHOW TIME

TIME TO STICK ON YOUR PYJAMAS, STAY UP PAST YOUR BEDTIME AND WATCH THE LATE LATE TOY SHOW!

Every year, Ryan Tubridy wears lots of different Christmas jumpers as he hosts the Toy Show.

Can you make this one as colourful and Christmassy as you can?

LIVING ROOM AUDITION

Have you ever wanted to present a toy on the *Late Late Toy Show*? Think you could do it better than the kids on the TV? Well, you can practise in your living room!

1. Get a toy you really like and round up an audience.

2. Introduce yourself – tell them where you're from, your age and your hobbies.

3. Describe your toy and tell your audience all the things you like and don't like about it.

TIP: Don't worry if your toy doesn't work, you forget your words or your sibling interrupts you – that's the whole point of the *Toy Show!*

PEANUT BUTTER CUPS

MAKES 6

120g peanut butter
1 tablespoon icing sugar
170g chocolate, melted
muffin tray
6 cupcake cases

1. Put the cupcake cases into a muffin tin.

2. Mix the peanut butter and icing sugar together until smooth.

3. Spread 1 tablespoon of chocolate on the bottom of each cupcake case.

4. Dollop 2 teaspoons of the peanut butter mixture on top of the chocolate.

5. Cover each dollop of peanut butter with 1 tablespoon of chocolate and smooth out the tops.

6. Refrigerate for 1 hour or until chocolate has hardened.

7. Peel off the liners and enjoy!

SMARTY PANTS!

The Toy Show started as a 30-minute slot in 1975 presented by Gay Byrne. Now it is watched by millions of people in over 100 countries around the world!

CHRISTMAS
SNOW PLACE LIKE HOME

YOU CAN MAKE YOUR OWN SNOWY SCENE WITH A FEW THINGS YOU HAVE AROUND THE HOUSE. ASK AN ADULT FOR HELP WITH THE GLUE!

TIP: Try different figurines to make your snow globe really unique. How about a dinosaur Christmas?

clean glass jar with a tight lid

plastic figurine

superglue

water

1 teaspoon glitter

1 tablespoon baby oil

1. Remove the lid from your jar and turn it upside-down. Glue your figurine in the centre and let it dry completely.

2. Fill the jar ¾ of the way with water, leaving a little room at the top.

3. Add a squirt of baby oil. This will make your 'snow' fall down more slowly.

4. Pour in the glitter – don't overdo it! Use a spoon to mix well.

5. Keeping the glass jar right-side up, put the lid on the jar and seal it tightly.

6. Turn it upside down and let it sit for a few minutes to make sure there are no leaks. You can add a little glue to the rim to make sure.

7. Gently shake your snow globe to create your own personal snowstorm!

YULE NEVER GUESS!

It's time for Christmas dinner! You're the chef and you need to cycle from the shop to your kitchen.

You have a **turkey**, a sack of **brussels sprouts** and your GAA-playing cousin **Michael**.

But your bike can only carry you and one other thing.

If you leave Michael with the turkey, the turkey will get eaten.

If you leave the turkey with the brussels sprouts, the sprouts will get eaten.

How will you get safely home with all three?

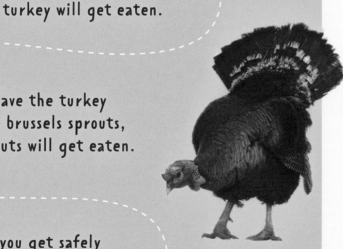

HINT:
You might have to make a few trips!

FOR CHRISTMAS, I WOULD LIKE...

1

2

3

SMARTY PANTS!

Depending on where you're from in the world, you might be visited by Kris Kringle, Papa Noël, Weihnachtsmann, Babbo Natale, Ded Moroz, Święty Mikołaj, Sinterklaas or Dun Che Lao Ren. But they're all different names for the same person – Santa Claus!

BiG QUiZ

How's your general knowledge? Were you paying attention this year? It's time to get **quizzical...**

ROUND 1

1. What is a baby kangaroo called?

2. How many sides does a pentagon have?

3. What are the names of Michael D. Higgins' dogs?

4. What does COVID-19 stand for?

5. Where would you find the Sea of Tranquility?

6. Who writes the *World's Worst* series of books?

7. Who is the captain of the Irish rugby team?

8. What movie, released in 2020, features an Irish boy genius and magical creatures?

ROUND 2

1. Rooster, Kerr's Pinks and Golden Wonders are all types of what?

2. What is the name of Harry Potter's owl?

3. What is a male deer called?

4. In what city would you find the Eiffel Tower?

5. What is Super Mario's brother called?

6. What is another name for the humerus bone?

7. What is the most sung song in the world?
   Hint: You probably had it sung to you this year.

8. In 2020, who led online PE classes for kids around the world?

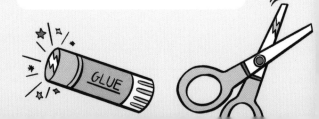

OF 2020!

ROUND 3

1. Woods, wedges and putters are all types of what?
2. In what country would you find the Taj Mahal?
3. Who has won the most All-Ireland Senior Football championships?
4. What does Tír na nÓg mean in English?
5. What is the largest organ in your body?
6. What is the name of the dog in *The Simpsons*?
7. What country is Greta Thunberg from?
8. Who became Taoiseach of Ireland in 2020?

ROUND 4

1. Mikado, Fig Roll and Bourbons are all types of what?
2. Name the three sports that make up a triathlon.
3. Which Irish county has the smallest population?
4. Where will the Olympics be held in 2021?
5. What are the most common monsters in Minecraft called?
6. How many pockets does a snooker table have?
7. What does the WHO stand for?
8. In 2020, *Wimpy Kid* author Jeff Kinney released a new book about Greg's best friend. What is his name?

ANSWERS

PAGE 8

1. Squirrel
2. Fox
3. Hedgehog
4. Duck
5. Deer
6. Mouse
7. Elephant
8. Sheep
9. Hare
10. Otter
11. Badger
12. Horse

PAGE 12

PAGE 16

1. Carrauntoohil
2. Louth
3. Lough Neagh
4. Leitrim
5. Phoenix Park
6. The Shannon

PAGE 17

1. Fungie the dolphin
2. Cliffs of Moher
3. Giant's Causeway
4. Blarney Stone
5. Temple Bar
6. Croagh Patrick
7. Bunratty Castle
8. Powerscourt Waterfall
9. English Market
10. Rock of Cashel

PAGE 21

Monitor
Games
Coding
Processor
Data
Memory
Hardware
Programmer
Network
Laptop
Console

PAGE 30

New Zealand: All Blacks
South Africa: Springboks
England: Red and Whites
Wales: Dragons
Ireland: Men in Green
Australia: Wallabies
France: Les Bleus
Argentina: Los Pumas
Scotland: Bravehearts
Japan: Brave Blossoms
Italy: Gli Azzurri

PAGE 32

1. **TRUE!** Honey is low in moisture and high in acid, so it won't spoil.
2. **FALSE!** They were developed in Australia to grow different types of fruit on one tree.
3. **FALSE!** They take two to three years to grow.
4. **TRUE!** Limes are slightly denser than lemons.
5. **TRUE!** White chocolate doesn't contain any cocoa beans.
6. **TRUE!** Wild bananas still exist, but the yellow ones we see in shops are all Cavendish clones.
7. **TRUE!** Those thieves must be pretty stinky.
8. **FALSE!** They're just painted rice cakes.
9. **FALSE!** They were paid in salt – that's where the word salary comes from.
10. **TRUE!** It's a sticky situation.

PAGE 35

Bono
Dermot Kennedy
Hozier
Niall Horan
The Script
Westlife
Picture This

PAGE 37

ACROSS
2. Wolf
7. Camel
8. Bat
9. Hedgehog
10. Panda
13. Giraffe
11. Crocodile
14. Kangaroo
16. Jellyfish

DOWN
1. Fox
3. Flamingo
4. Zebra
5. Leopard
6. Cheetah
12. Whale
15. Owl

PAGE 40

ACROSS
2. Strait
6. Canada
9. Nigeria
10. Seine
11. Brazil

DOWN
1. Peru
2. Syria
3. Tokyo
4. Ganges
5. Hawaii
7. Mariana
8. Andes

PAGE 50

1. **FALSE!** It was named after Thomas Croke, who was an archbishop.
2. **TRUE!** The hungry seagulls come looking for dropped food.
3. **TRUE!** The Republic of Ireland took on Wales in this historical match.
4. **TRUE!** He fought and beat Al 'Blue' Lewis.
5. **FALSE!** The weather was so awful it was called the Thunder and Lightning Final. World War II also broke out that day.
6. **TRUE!** These days, €3,500 will get you a luxury annual membership.
7. **FALSE!** It's twice the size.
8. **FALSE!** There are more than 400.
9. **TRUE!** The originals are kept safe in the GAA Museum.
10. **FALSE!** It's 17 storeys high. You can take a tour, if you dare.

PAGE 56-57

ROUND 1
1. Joey
2. Five
3. Bród and Síoda
4. Coronavirus Disease 2019
5. The moon
6. David Walliams
7. Johnny Sexton
8. Artemis Fowl

ROUND 2
1. Potatoes
2. Hedwig
3. Stag
4. Paris
5. Luigi
6. Funny bone
7. Happy Birthday
8. Joe Wicks

ROUND 3
1. Golf clubs
2. India
3. Kerry
4. Land of the young
5. Your skin
6. Santa's Little Helper
7. Sweden
8. Micheál Martin

ROUND 4
1. Biscuits
2. Running, cycling and swimming
3. Leitrim
4. Tokyo
5. Creepers
6. Six
7. World Health Organization
8. Rowley Jefferson

SMARTY PANTS!

Gill Books
Hume Avenue
Park West
Dublin 12
www.gillbooks.ie

Gill Books is an imprint of M.H. Gill and Co.

© Gill Books 2020

978 0717 18998 4

Text by Sheila Armstrong
Designed by grahamthew.com
Print origination by Sarah McCoy
Illustrations by Jacky Sheridan
Printed by Hussar Books, Poland

For permission to reproduce photographs, the authors and publisher gratefully acknowledge the following:

© Alamy: 11T, 12, 19TR, 19BR, 28TL, 28B, 58; © Brendan Moran/Getty Images: 50T; © Danny Martindale/Getty Images: 14; © Dublin Zoo: 36, 37BL, 37BR; © Freepik: 7B, 11B, 15T, 15B, 23, 28TR, 32R, 33T, 33B, 34TL, 49, 53T; © Hulton Archive via Getty: 2C; © iStock/Getty Premium: 2TL, 3T, 3B, 5L, 5C, 5R, 6, 7T, 9T, 9BL, 9BC, 10, 16, 17, 19TR, 19TC, 19BL, 19TC, 22TR, 22BL, 22BR, 27, 29, 32L, 34TR, 35L, 35R, 37T, 41TR, 41BR, 48B, 50CT, 53C, 54, 55L, 55R; © RTÉ: 52, 53B; © Shutterstock: 30a, 41L, 50CB; © WikiCommons: 2TR, 2BL, 2BR, 30c, 30d, 30e, 30f, 44, 51L, 51R; image courtesy of Chorusman/WikiCommons: 50B; image courtesy of Jonathan Tallon/WikiCommons: 51C; image courtesy of The Royal Society: 38; image courtesy of Warwick Gastinger/WikiCommons: 30b; illustrations courtesy of Freepik: 1BR, 2, 3T, 4CR, 5B, 7C, 8C, 9, 10C, 10BL, 11T, 11C, 12, 13B, 14T, 18, 19T, 22CL, 22BR, 23, 26C, 27TL, 29TC, 33BR, 35TR, 38, 39CR, 39BR, 40T, 40B, 41T, 48, 49B, 52B, 54CR, 55TC.

This book is typeset in Neue Kabel and Tomarik.

A CIP catalogue record for this book is available from the British Library.

5 4 3 2 1